JOHN W. SCHAUM
DUET ALBUM

BOOK TWO

JOHN W. SCHAUM

Born in Milwaukee, Wisconsin. Founder and Director of the famous Schaum Piano School at Milwaukee. Mus. M., Northwestern University; Mus. B., Marquette University; B. Ed., Milwaukee Teachers' College; Unlimited state certificate to teach piano; 12 seasons on Shorewood Opportunity School Faculty; 9 years head of Piano Department at Milwaukee University School; soloist with Milwaukee Philharmonic Orchestra. Past President of Wisconsin Music Teachers' Association; Composer of many Original Compositions for the Piano. Editor and arranger of more than 300 Standard Pieces and Supplementary Books for the Young Piano Student. Composer of the famous "Schaum Note Speller" and the "Schaum Piano Course."

Lithographed in U.S.A.

CONTENTS

Ed. Libr. No. 216

FOREWORD

The *John W. Schaum Duet Album* contains several highlights which offer definite contributions to piano teaching:—

1. The measures of each duet are numbered identically enabling the players to know instantly where to re-start in case a mistake is made.

2. The duets are arranged for two pupils to play. The primos and secondos are of equal difficulty so that the pupils can freely alternate between the two parts. The old-fashioned duets designed for teacher and pupil were discouragingly hard for the pupils who wanted to try both parts. The *John W. Schaum Duet Album* will have a wholesome effect on the mental attitude of the pupil who likes to explore.

3. Parents will be encouraged to play ensemble with their children because the parts are of equal difficulty. Many parents have had only a modest musical education and would be unable to perform a difficult teacher's part. Parents will appreciate the *Schaum Duet Album*.

4. The selections are based on familiar folk songs and famous classics. For added flavor, one of the duets has been seasoned with a dash of ballroom rhythm. This wide variety of material gives the players experience in many styles and rhythms.

5. These duets will add novelty and zest to any recital program.

Ed. Libr. No. 216

DIXIE DOODLE

Secondo

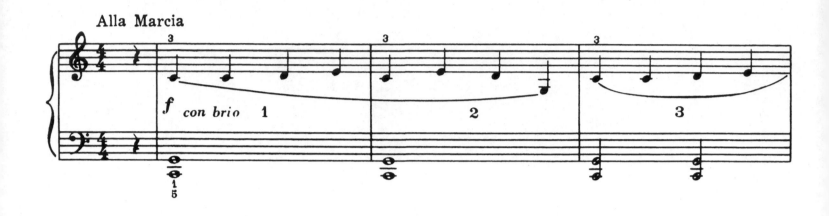

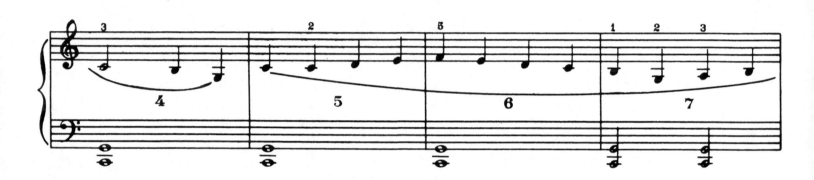

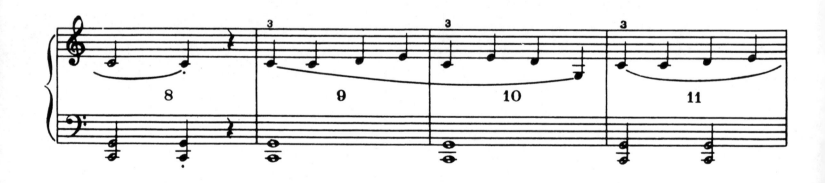

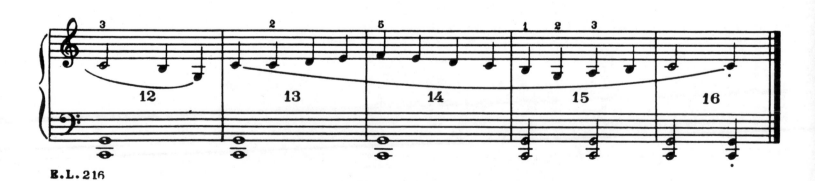

E.L. 216

DIXIE DOODLE

Primo

Note: This duet combines Yankee Doodle in the secondo with Dixie in the primo. Hence, the title: Dixie Doodle.

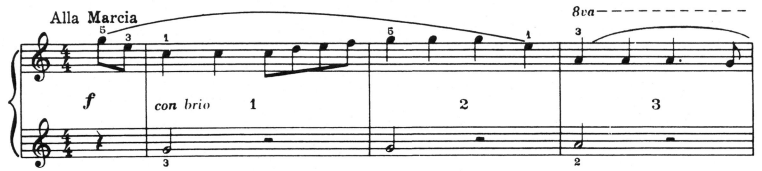

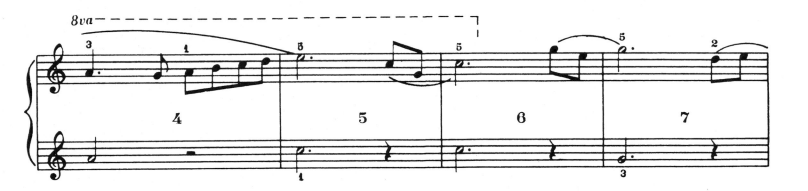

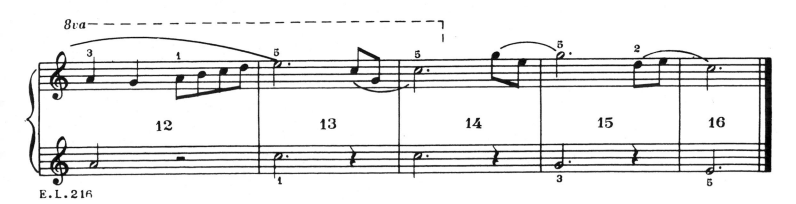

E.L.216

CAMPUS CAPERS

Secondo

CAMPUS CAPERS

Primo

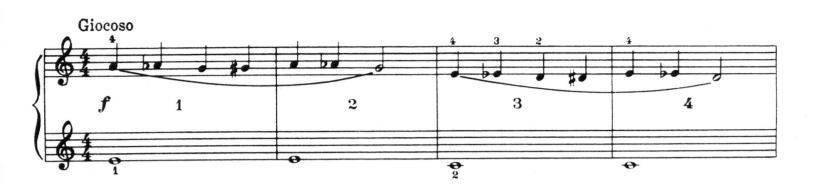

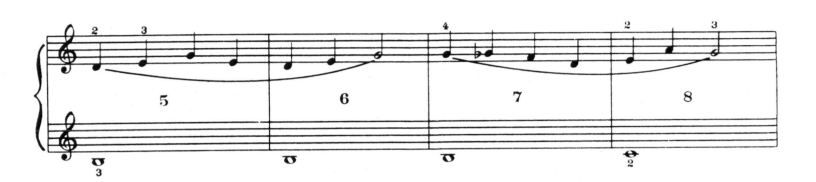

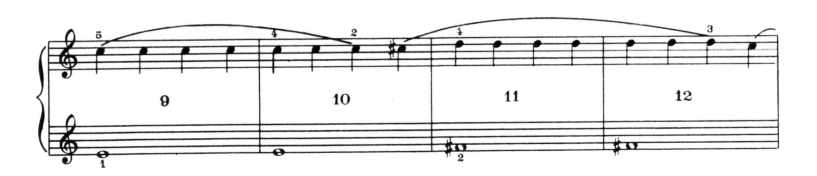

Sheet Music Duet

Bicycle Built for Two (H. Dacre) Arr. by John W. Schaum

E.L. 216

Secondo

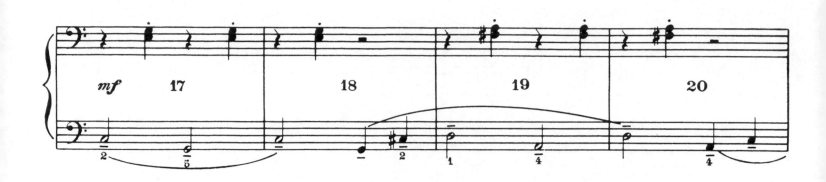

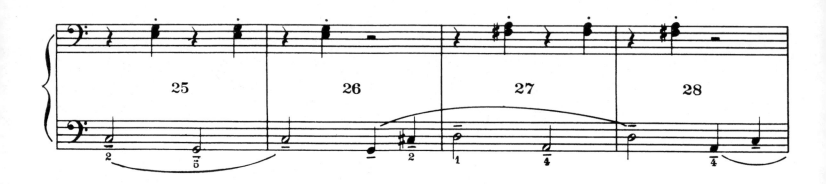

E.L. 216

Primo

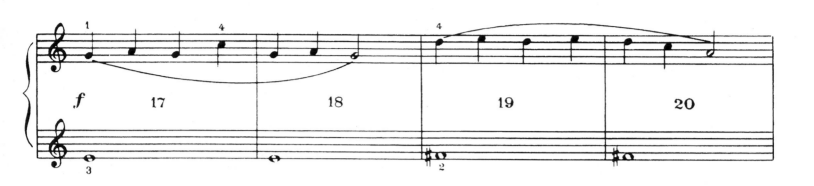

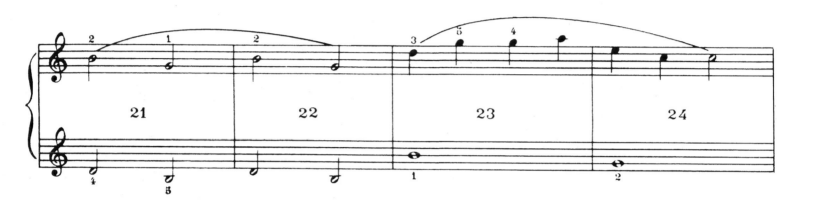

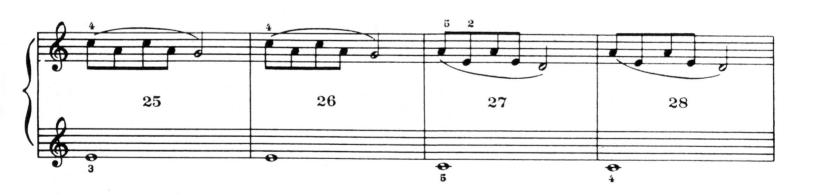

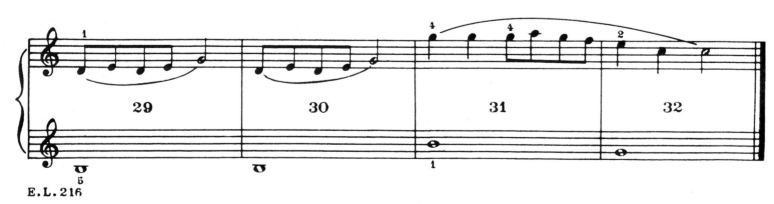

E.L.216

ROCKIN' IN THE ROCKIES

Secondo

TRADITIONAL

Allegro

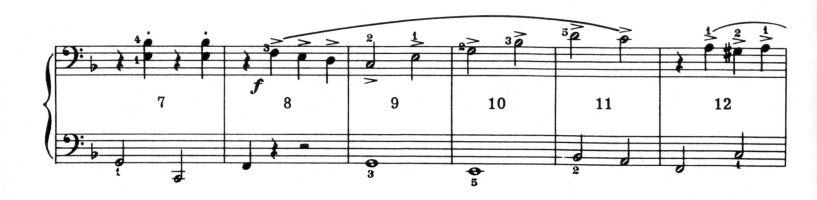

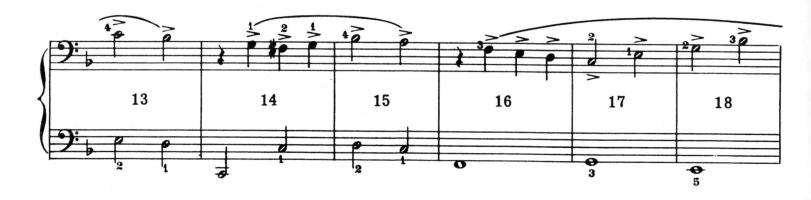

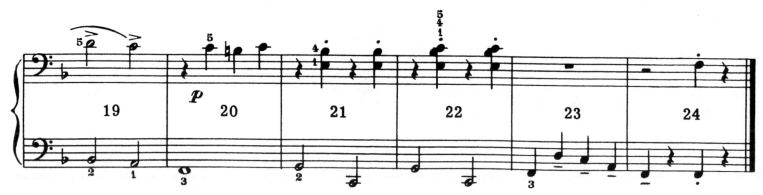

EL 216

ROCKIN' IN THE ROCKIES

Primo

TRADITIONAL

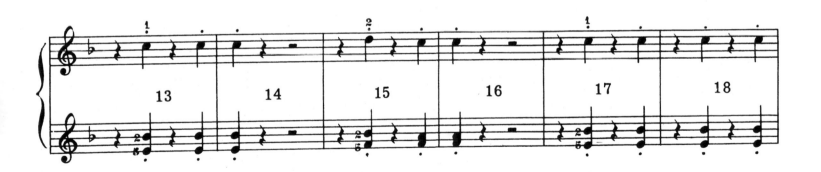

TURKISH RONDO

Secondo

W. A. MOZART

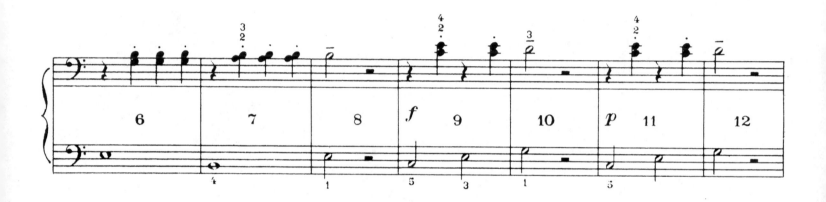

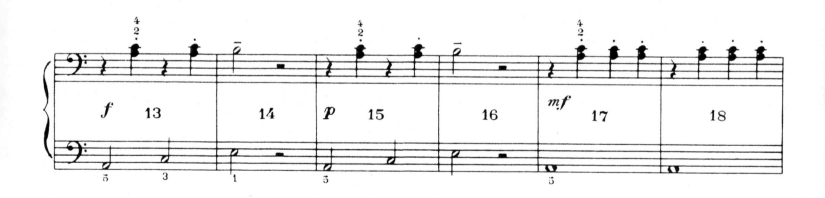

E. L. 216

TURKISH RONDO

Primo

W. A. MOZART

MEMORIES OF JOHANN STRAUSS

Secondo

Tempo di Valse
Intro.

ARTIST'S LIFE

MEMORIES OF JOHANN STRAUSS

Primo

THE BLUE DANUBE

THE BLUE DANUBE

COUNTRY GARDENS

Secondo

COUNTRY GARDENS

Primo

E.L. 216

MINUET IN G
Secondo

J S. BACH

MINUET IN G
Primo

J S. BACH

THE ANGELUS

Secondo

Moderato

CHARLES GOUNOD

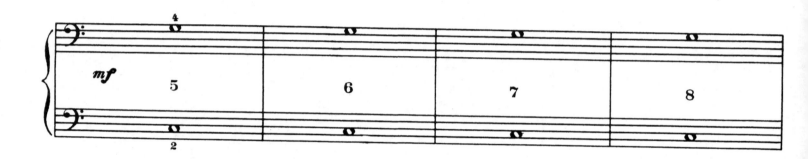

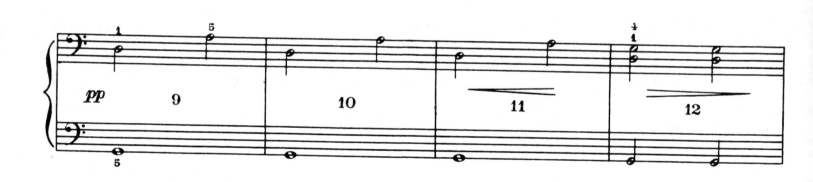

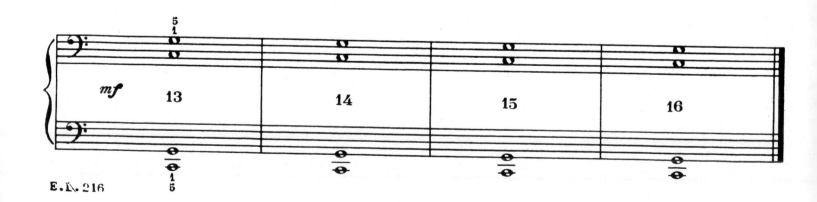

THE ANGELUS
Primo

CHARLES GOUNOD

Note: This duet was especially composed by Gounod for his nieces: Charlotte and Therese Gounod.

SHADOW WALTZ

from "Dinorah"

Secondo

G. MEYERBEER

SHADOW WALTZ

from "Dinorah"

Primo

G. MEYERBEER

THE DANCING STARLET

Secondo

Allegretto con anima

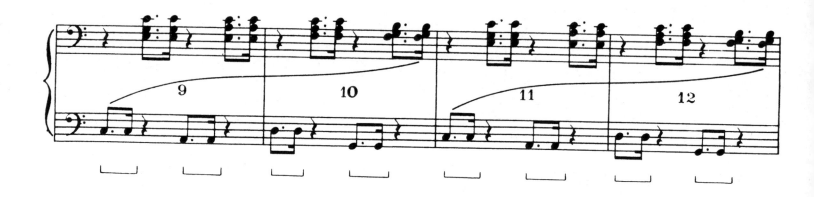

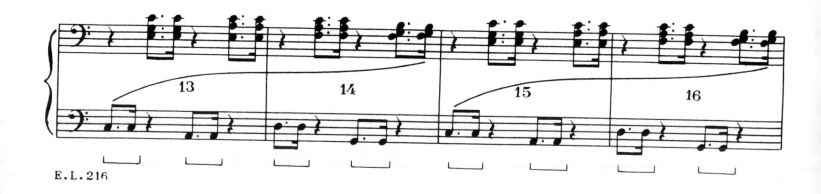

THE DANCING STARLET

Primo

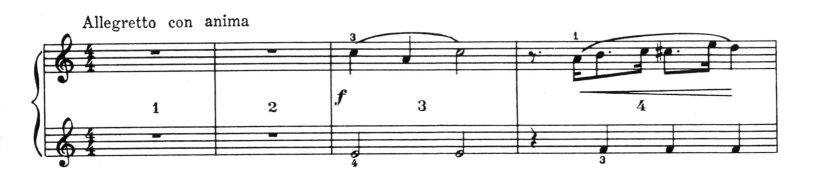

E.L.216

Secondo

Primo

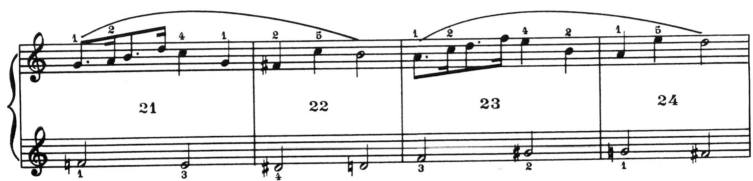

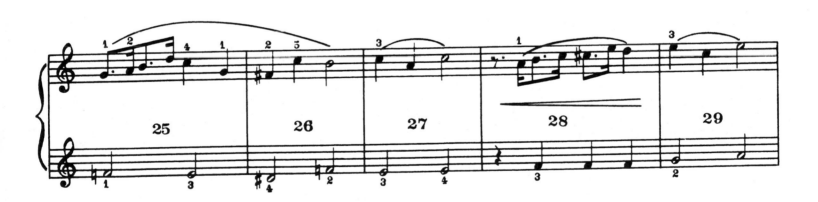

E. L. 216

MARCH from TANNHAUSER

Secondo

RICHARD WAGNER

MARCH from TANNHAUSER

Primo

Andante alla Marcia

RICHARD WAGNER